Know About
Ashoka the Great

MAPLE KIDS

KNOW ABOUT ASHOKA THE GREAT

ALL RIGHTS RESERVED. No part of this book may be reproduced in a retrieval system or transmitted in any form or by any means electronics, mechanical, photocopying, recording and or without permission of the publisher.

Published by

MAPLE PRESS PRIVATE LIMITED
office: A-63, Sector 58, Noida 201301, U.P., India
phone: +91 120 455 3581, 455 3583
email: info@maplepress.co.in
website: www.maplepress.co.in

Reprinted in 2019

ISBN: 978-93-50334-04-1

Contents

Preface 4
1. Ashoka - An Overview 6
2. The Mauryan Empire 9
3. Seleucus Invasion 13
4. Bindusara 17
5. The Devanampriya Priyadarshi 20
6. The Revolt at Taxila 22
7. Ashoka Becomes King 25
8. The Kalinga War 27
9. Conquer Kalinga 29
10. Laying Down Arms 31
11. Ashoka and Buddhism 35
12. The Basics of Buddhism 39
13. Spreading the Message of Dharma 44
14. The Able Ruler 47
15. The Seeds of Dharma 51
16. The Buddhist Council 53
17. The Second Pilgrimage 56
18. The People's Friend 58
19. The Proficient Ruler 63
20. The Last Days 65
21. The Generous King 67
22. The Decline of Mauryan Empire 71
23. Ashoka the Shining Star 74
24. Edicts of Ashok 76

Preface

"There is no better work than promoting the welfare of the world. Whatever be my great deeds, I have done them in order to discharge my debt to all beings."

These words were spoken by Ashoka, the third emperor of the illustrious Mauryan dynasty of India and one of the most powerful kings of the Indian subcontinent in ancient times. His reign between 273 B.C. and 232 B.C. was one of the most prosperous periods in the history of India.

Lord of a vast empire, after a great victory on the battlefield of Kalinga, felt overwhelmed with the brutality of his actions after seeing the destruction around after the war and took an oath never to fight again. He was an ideal ruler who strove to carry to other lands, the enlightenment that he had attained in his life. He dedicated himself to the victories of righteousness. Ashoka without doubt was one of the most humanitarian rulers that ruled over the country, India.

Apart from this, he is also famous for his edicts and stupas, which form a part of ancient architecture of India.

The Wheel, which adorns the flag of free India, has kept his memory green.

This book is about the life and times of the greatest conqueror, who conquered not with arms but with love.

CHAPTER 1
Ashoka - An Overview

Ashoka (also sometimes transliterated as 'Asoka'), the grandson of Chandragupta - the founder of the Mauryan dynasty - and the son of Bindusara, came to the throne circa 268 B.C. and died approximately 233 B.C. He is chiefly known from his series of rock and pillar inscriptions, which are found, scattered in various parts of India and provide important information about his reign and policies. After eight years of rule, he waged a fierce war against the kingdom of Kalinga (Orissa of today) and was so horrified at the carnage he had caused that he gave up violence and turned to Buddhism.

In his efforts to propagate Buddhism, Ashoka built shrines and monasteries and inscribed Buddhist teachings on rocks and pillars in many places. He sent missionaries to countries as remote as Greece and Egypt. His own son, a monk, carried Buddhism to Sri Lanka, where it is still the major religion. Despite Ashoka's vigorous exertions of faith, he was tolerant of other religions. The empire enjoyed remarkable prosperity during his reign.

Some Indian historians think that his policy of peace led to the downfall of the Mauryan Empire, which fell apart after his death.

He was soon largely forgotten by Indian tradition and only remembered in Buddhist circles as a great patron of the faith. With the deciphering of his inscriptions during the 19th century, he took his rightful place in world history as one of the most benevolent rulers of antiquity.

King Ashoka was responsible for a number of Buddhist monuments. The splendid monolithic stone pillars on which many of his inscriptions are engraved, are among the masterpieces of Indian art, and the capital atop one of them, the Sarnath Pillar, inspired the use of back-to-back lions, that is the Indian national emblem. The 24-spoked Ashoka-chakra, which has found its way into the Indian national flag is also found artifact of Ashoka's period.

CHAPTER 2
The Mauryan Empire

Ashoka belonged to the illustrious Mauryan dynasty that was established by the great King Chandragupta Maurya.

Chandragupta Maurya succeeded the Nanda throne in 321 B.C. He was then a young man of about 25 and was the ally of the Brahmin Chanakya (also known as Kautilya), who was also his guide and mentor, both in acquiring the throne and in retaining it. The acquisition of Magadha was the first step in establishing the new dynasty. Chandragupta belonged to the Moriya tribe, a Kshatriya (warrior) clan of a little ancient republic of Pippalivana, situated between Rummindei (Nepali Tarai) and Kasia (Gorakhpur district of Uttar Pradesh). It is also claimed that Chandragupta Maurya was abandoned by his parents. According to the legend, he was raised by a pastoral family and then was later sheltered by Chanakya, who taught him the rules of administration and everything else that is required for one to become a successful emperor. Young Maurya and his supporters were inferior in armed strength to the Nandas. However, it was here that Kautilya's strategy played a significant role in defeating the Nanda Kingdom. They began by harassing the outlying areas of the Nanda kingdom, gradually moving towards the centre, this strategy being based on the morale drawn from the fact that the Kautilya saw a woman scolding her child for eating from the centre of the dish, since the centre was bound to be much hotter than the sides. Once the Ganges valley was under his control, Kautilya now advised Chandragupta to move to the north-west, to exploit the power vacuum created by Alexander's departure. The areas of the north-west fell to him rapidly until he reached the Indus. Here, he paused for the moment, as the Greek Seleucid dynasty had fortified itself in Persia and was determined to hold the trans Indus region.

Chandragupta moved to Central India for a while and occupied the region north of the Narmada River. But 305 B.C. saw him back in the north-west, involved in a campaign against Seleucus Nicator, which Chandragupta finally won in 303 B.C. The Seleucid provinces of trans Indus, which today would cover large parts of Afghanistan, were ceded to the Mauryas. The territorial foundation of the Mauryan Empire had been laid, with Chandragupta controlling the Indus and the Ganges plain and the far north-west - a formidable empire by Indian standards.

Despite the campaign against Seleucids, there was considerable contact of a friendly nature between the two civilizations. Sandrocottos (Chandragupta) is frequently

referred to in the Greek accounts. The treaty of 303 B.C. also included a marriage between Seleucus's daughter Helen and Chandragupta Maurya. Seleucus's ambassador Megasthenes accompanied Chandragupta to his court and gave an interesting and informative account about him and Kautilya.

Towards the end of his life, Chandragupta converted to Jainism and he abdicated in favour of his son, Bindusara and became an ascetic. Together with one of the Jain saints and many other monks, he went to south India, and there, he ended his life by deliberate slow starvation in the orthodox Jain manner.

CHAPTER 3
Seleucus Invasion

Alexander died in 323 B.C. Seleucus was one of the leading generals of Alexander. While journeying back to Greece from India, when Alexander reached Babylon, he fell seriously ill and died there in 323 B.C. Alexander died without any heir. So, his extensive empire was shared out by his three Generals among themselves. Thus, the far-flung empire of Alexander was split up into three parts- the Greek, the Egyptian and the Asian. The first two parts came into the possession of Ptolemy and Antigones respectively, while the third, i.e. the Asian part, fell to the lot of Seleucus. Seleucus's Asian empire extended from Syria up to the Euphrates. He also held some parts of Punjab and Afghanistan. Seleucus had accompanied Alexander during his invasion of India in 326 B.C. After the death of Alexander in 323 B.C., Chandragupta Maurya had established a strong empire in India and had driven out the Greeks from the Indian soil. Seleucus therefore wanted to regain these territories and to move further to the east of Indus.

The coronation of the Mauryan emperor, Chandragupta, took place in 321 B.C., two years after Alexander had left India. He united the country into a strong and well-knit empire. With the help of his able minister and astute diplomat Kautilya, he succeeded in laying the foundation of a strong empire. The image of India, which Seleucus had formed in his mind, was that of a country fragmented into small kingdoms and was prone to mutual rivalries and jealousies. He, therefore, entertained the ambition of conquest of India, but little did he knew that India, which he was going to face, was even more powerful than his own empire. Consequently, Seleucus advanced with a huge army against India in 305 B.C. The Indian soldiers were in fine fettle and their horsemen, chariot army and elephants were ready to inflict defeat on the invaders. A terrible war followed on the north-west borders of India. The Greeks could not withstand the onslaught of the gallant Indian fighters. The army of Chandragupta Maurya routed the invaders and Seleucus was forced to sign a peace treaty. Chandragupta Maurya, advised by Kautilya, presented his terms to the defeated army. Seleucus was forced to accept. By the terms of the treaty, Seleucus surrendered his territories in Afghanistan - Herat, Kandhar and the Kabul valley - to Chandragupta Maurya. In return, he was presented the gift of 300 elephants. On Kautilya's advice, Chandragupta married the daughter of Seleucus, Helen. Seleucus also appointed Megasthenes as his ambassador to the Mauryan court. Megasthenes wrote a famous account of his stay at the Mauryan court in a book entitled *Indica*.

Besides the preponderant army and armaments, one factor that contributed to the victory of Chandragupta Maurya in this war was that, as a result of Alexander's invasion, Indians had also become familiar with the Greek methods of warfare. Moreover, it was by dint of his bravery and Kautilya's sharp intelligence that Chandragupta Maurya had built up such an extensive empire. His vast army was also well-trained and well-equipped.

Little is known of the campaign, in which Chandragupta fought with Seleucus over the Indus Valley and the region of Gandhara. The Greek historians have also confined themselves to just mentioning its results. From the results, however, we can draw this conclusion that Seleucus certainly sustained a crushing defeat in the war, and his dream of the conquest of India was shattered forever.

CHAPTER 4
Bindusara

Chandragupta was succeeded by his son Bindusara in 297 B.C. To the Greeks, Bindusara was known as Amitrochates, perhaps the Greek translation of the Sanskrit Amitraghata means the destroyer of the foes.

Apparently, he was a man of wide interest and taste. It is known from the Greek accounts that Bindusara once requested the Syrian King Antiochus I Soter, who was the son of Seleucus Nicator, to send him some sweet wine, dried figs and a sophist. Bindusara campaigned in the Deccan, extending the Mauryan Empire in the peninsula to as far as Mysore. He is said to have conquered 'the land between the two seas', presumably the Arabian Sea and the Bay of Bengal.

Early Tamil poets speak of Mauryan chariots thundering across the land, their white pennants brilliant in the sunshine. At the time of Bindusara's death in 272 B.C., practically the entire sub-continent had come under Mauryan suzerainty. The extreme south was ready to submit, thus eliminating the need for military conquest. Yet, one area alone remained hostile and unconquered, Kalinga, on the east coast (modern Orissa). This was left to Bindusara's son Ashoka, who campaigned successfully against Kalinga.

Subhadrangi was the mother of Ashoka. She was the daughter of poor Brahmin of Champakanagar. There is an interesting story about the birth of Ashoka.

A Brahmin belonging to Champa city in his kingdom had a very beautiful daughter named Subhadrangi. Once, his home was visited by an astrologer, who foretold that one day his daughter would be the queen of a great king, ruling over the whole continent.

When she grew up, the Brahmin adorned her with all the ornaments he possessed and came to the King Bindusara who accepted Brahmin's daughter in his inner apartments. The young girl was so beautiful, which excited the jealousy of the other queens. They became apprehensive about the fact that if the king would get a chance of her glimpse, then he would never look at any of them. Therefore, they contrived a plan. They taught her the barber's art, and sent her to groom the hair and beard of Bindusara. But, the plan failed. She did her work in such a way that the king still got attracted towards her.

Extremely pleased with her, Bindusara one day asked her what she would like most of all. She asked for a son. "But how can I, a Kshatriya monarch, marry a barber's girl!" said the king. "Your Majesty," she replied, "I am not a barber girl, but the daughter of a Brahmin. My father gifted me to your highness as a wife." Finding out who had taught her the barber's art, the king passed orders that she would not do so any longer. Instead, as his queens had feared, he installed her as his Chief Queen.

After sometime, she gave birth to a son in 294 B.C. When the king asked her about the name of the child, she immediately replied 'Ashoka'.

CHAPTER 5
The Devanampriya Priyadarshi

"All men are my children. I am like a father to them. As every father desires the good and the happiness of his children, I wish that all men should be happy always."

These are the words of an emperor who lived two thousand and three hundred years ago.

We see in history, how, even mere chieftains grew arrogant and used their powers selfishly and unjustly. But, the emperor who said the a bove words ruled over the greater part of India. He had the power of life and death over millions of his subjects.

Is it surprising that free India remembers him with admiration?

This emperor was no other than Ashoka who is also called 'Devanampriya Priyadarshi'.

Who was 'Priyadarshi'?

The rock inscriptions of Devanampriya Priyadarshi were being discovered all over India for centuries. But for a

long time, the identity of this 'Devanampriya Priyadarshi' remained a puzzle.

One day, in the year 1915, near a village called Maski in Raichur District of Karnataka, a rock inscription was discovered on a hill. In this inscription, for the first time, the name of Ashoka was found with titles Devanampriya ("the Beloved of the Gods") and Priyadarshi ("He who regards everyone with affection"). It was then certain that Devanampriya Priyadarshi was none other than Ashoka the Mauryan Emperor, whose name shines like a very bright star in the history of the world, and whom the world honours and loves even two thousand years after his death.

CHAPTER 6
The Revolt at Taxila

As a boy, Ashoka was not only active but also mischievous. He was a skilful hunter. From the time of Chandragupta Maurya, the hunting expedition of the Emperor and the royal family was a splendid sight.

Ashoka was not handsome. But no prince excelled him in valour, courage, dignity, love of adventure and ability in administration. Therefore, even as a prince, Ashoka was loved and respected by his subjects and his ministers. Bindusara discovered the ability of his son quite early and, when Ashoka was still young, appointed him Governor of Avanti.

Ujjain was the capital of Avanti. It was a beautiful city, and the home of knowledge, wealth and art. Within a few days of taking over the administration of Avanti, Ashoka became an excellent statesman. It was, when he was in this city that he married Shakya Kumari, the beautiful daughter of a merchant of Vidishanagar. She gave birth to two children, Mahendra and Sanghamitra.

Ashoka's valour, courage and wisdom were soon tested.

When prince Ashoka was working as the viceroy at Ujjain, prince Sushima, the eldest son of Bindusara, was serving as his father's viceroy at Taxila. During that period, a revolt of the people of Taxila broke out due to the misdeeds of the wicked officers under Sushima's administration. Sushima failed to put down the rebellion. Bindusara sent Ashoka to suppress the revolt. Ashoka did not have enough forces but yet moved towards the city boldly.

A surprising thing happened. The citizens of Taxila never thought of fighting against Ashoka. They gave him a grand welcome. They pleaded, "We do not hate either Bindusara or the royal family. The wicked ministers are responsible for our revolt. We misunderstood you because of their evil advice. We are not rebels. Please forgive us."

Ashoka understood the real situation and punished those responsible for the revolt. He stayed there for some days and gave the people some advice in simple and beautiful words. When complete peace was established in the city, Ashoka returned to his province.

Days and years passed. Bindusara grew old. His body became weak. His health declined.

Among his ministers, one of them by the name Radhagupta was prominent. He and the others began to think about the future welfare of the empire.

Bindusara's eldest son was Sushima. According to custom, he should have succeeded to the throne. But the revolt of Taxila had exposed his weakness.

Besides, he had begun to behave with insolence.

The council of ministers felt that the empire would suffer and would lose peace and prosperity, also there would be no justice in the land if Sushima were crowned king. Therefore, they sent word to Ashoka that his father was ill and that he should rush to the bedside of his sick father.

CHAPTER 7
Ashoka Becomes King

Emperor Bindusara died in 272 B.C. Ashoka who had come to Pataliputra from Ujjain at the request of Radhagupta, the Chief Minister, was crowned king of Magadha after the death of his father.

What happened after this is not very clear. Perhaps, Sushima heard the news of his father's death and feared that Ashoka might be crowned King, he probably came from Taxila with a large army. He came prepared to fight if necessary. But, he was killed, even as he was attempting to gain an entrance to the city.

It is mentioned in Buddhist literature that Ashoka had almost killed all his brothers for the sake of the kingdom. Among all his brothers he only spared his younger brother Vithashoka. There is no historical basis for this story. Ashoka has spoken affectionately about his brothers in his rock inscriptions. The fifth day of the third month Jyestamasa, of the year 268 B.C. was the auspicious day on which Ashoka was crowned king. Pataliputra was gaily decorated. The auspicious time fixed for the coronation arrived. Auspicious music was sounded. The young and radiant Ashoka entered the court, surrounded by his bodyguards. The heir to the throne of Magadha bowed to the throne and ascended it. As the priests chanted sacred verses, the heir was adorned with the appropriate symbols of royalty and the crown was placed on his head. The citizens of Pataliputra rejoiced that the empire was blessed with an able ruler.

Ashoka was a very intelligent statesman. He ruled over Magadha wisely and ably. The council of ministers and officers of state were obedient, dutiful and able. Therefore, peace and abundance brightened the land. Eight years passed with happiness and peace under Ashoka's ruling.

CHAPTER 8
The Kalinga War

When Ashoka ascended the throne of Magadha in 273 B.C., treading in the footsteps of his forefathers, he set out to expand his empire. In the 12th year of his reign, he sent a message to Kalinga asking its submission, but the Kalingaraj refused to submit to the Mauryan Empire.

As a result, Ashoka led a huge army against Kalinga. This took place in 261 B.C, the freedom loving people of Kalinga offered a stiff resistance to the Mauryan army. The whole of Kalinga turned into a battle arena. History offers us but few examples of such fiercely fought wars as this. The Kalingaraj himself commanded his army in the battlefield. However, the limited force of Kalinga was no match for the overwhelming Magadha army. Contrary to Ashoka's expectations, the people of Kalinga fought with such great valour that on a number of occasions, they came very close to a victory. The soldiers of Kalinga perished in the battlefield, fighting till their last breath for their independence. The victory ultimately rested with Ashoka.

The war took a tremendous toll of life and property. The 13th rock edict of Ashoka throws light on this war. At least 0.1 million Kalingans were killed, while another 0.15 million were taken prisoners. And almost equal numbers of Magadha soldiers were also killed. There was not a single man left in Kalinga to live a life of slavery.

This is the singular instance of a war in history, which brought about a complete change of heart in a stern ruler like Ashoka. The scene of the war presented a horrible sight, the whole terrain was covered with the corpses of soldiers, wounded soldiers groaning in severe pain, vultures hovered over their dead bodies, orphaned children mourning the loss of their near and dear ones, widows looked blank and despaired.

This sight overwhelmed Ashoka. He realised that his victory at such a cost is not worthwhile to the mankind. He left Kalinga to Pataliputra with a heavy heart.

CHAPTER 9
Conquer Kalinga

After having defeated Kalinga in the war, Ashoka decided to bring the kingdom under his control. He made it a point that he would rule Kalinga as he ruled his other subjects.

He then appointed officers to administer the kingdom. He knew that, as per the customs of those days, the officers who went from the victorious state to the defeated land usually treated the people of the defeated kingdom with scorn and contempt. They lost all sense of justice and fair play and behaved proudly. They insulted the defeated people. Ashoka did not want this to happen. He desired that the people of Kalinga should live in peace and honour. This was his order to the officers who were sent to Kalinga, "I have put you in charge of thousands of people. Earn the love and affection of all those people. Whatever situation may arise, treat all people alike. Be impartial in your actions. Give up rudeness, haste, laziness, lack of interest and short temper. Nothing can be achieved if we are bored and idle. Therefore, be active. If you understand how sacred your work is and if you behave with a sense of responsibility, you will go to heaven, and you will also repay your debt to the king who appointed you." Ashoka who treated his subjects as his children, further said, "Like a mother who gives her child to an able nurse, trusting that she would bring up the baby well. I have entrusted my subjects to your care."

Ashoka was really a great philanthropist who worked day and night for the welfare of his people. He knew exactly what was going on in each part of his vast territory and kept himself away of all the activities that were talking in the vanquished Kalinga.

Kalinga Stupa

Ashoka built the Dhauli Shanti Stupa at Kalinga, which commemorates the historic leap of faith that Emperor Ashoka went through in the aftermath of the famous Battle of Kalinga, 261 B.C, which changed Chandashoka (Ashoka, the Hawk) to Dharmashoka (Ashoka, the Dove) overnight.

CHAPTER 10
Laying Down Arms

Ashoka became the lord of Kalinga as he had wished. But, the victory brought him not joy but grief. The sights of grim slaughter he had seen, dimmed the pride of victory. Whether Ashoka was resting, sleeping or awake, the scenes of agony and death, he had seen on the battlefield, haunted him at all times, he could not have peace of mind even for a moment.

Ashoka understood that the flames of war not only burn and destroy on the battlefield but also spread to other fields and destroy many innocent lives.

The suffering caused by war does not end on the battlefield, it continues to poison the minds and lives of the survivors for a long time. At this time, Ashoka was at the height of his power, he was the head of a vast empire and had no equal in wealth or armed strength. And yet, the Kalinga war, which was his first war, also became his last war! The power of arms bowed before the power of Dharma (righteousness).

Ashoka swore that he would never again take to arms and that he would never again commit such a crime against humanity. And, it proved to be the oath of a man of iron.

In the history of the world, many kings have sworn not to fight again, after they had been defeated.

But, how many kings have been moved by pity in the hour of victory and laid down arms? Perhaps, there has been only one such king in the history of the whole world- Ashoka. The victory of Dharma brings with it love and affection. Devanampriya believes that, however small may be the love gained by its victory, it brings ample reward in the other world.

The whole war resulted in Ashoka's devotion towards Buddhism and after two and a half years, he became an

ardent follower of Buddhism under the guidance of one of Buddha's disciples Acharya Upagupta. The teaching of Buddha brought peace to Ashoka who was haunted by memories of the agony he had seen in Kalinga. Buddha's message of non-violence, kindness and love of mankind appealed to the unhappy Ashoka. Ashoka's heart now became the home of compassion, right living, love and nonviolence. He gave up hunting and eating meat. He put an end to the killing of animals for the royal kitchen. Realising that it was not enough if he lived a righteous life, he proclaimed that all his subjects also should live a life of righteousness.

Throughout his life, 'Ashoka the Great' followed the policy of non-violence or ahimsa. The slaughter or mutilation of animals was abolished in his kingdom. He promoted the concept of vegetarianism. The caste system ceased to exist in his eyes and he treated all his subjects as equals. At the same time, each and every person was given the rights to freedom, tolerance, and equality.

Ashoka now realised that, 'Of all victories, the victory of Dharma is the noblest. One may win a piece of land by fighting a war. But by kindness, love and pity, one can win the hearts of people. The sharp point of the sword spills blood, but from Dharma springs the fountain of love. The victory won by arms brings fleeting joy, but the victory of Dharma brings lasting joy'.

So, he taught his subjects this lesson, "All people should live a life of truthfulness, justice and love. Respect your parents. Treat your teachers and relatives with affection. Be modest in their presence. Give charity. Do not be unkind to animals. No one should think that he and his religion are the greatest. All religions preach the same virtues. Just as it is bad to indulge in self-praise and slandering others, it is bad to condemn other religions. Respect for other religions brings glory to one's own religion."

CHAPTER 11
Ashoka and Buddhism

Though it is generally believed that Acharya initiated Ashoka into Buddhism, yet there are various speculations regarding the initiation of Ashoka into Buddhism. One of the stories says that after the battle of Kalinga when Ashoka was going through a trauma, a Buddhist monk named Samudra arrived in Pataliputra. Unknowingly, he stepped into the imposing mansion, 'The Paradisal Hell', (Ashoka's Hell) asking for alms. Ashoka's Hell is an elaborate torture chamber disguised as a beautiful palace full of amenities. Samudra did not see a very pleasant sight inside the palace and tried to leave the mansion immediately, but Chandagirikaa stopped him. "This is where your life ends," said the royal executioner and was surprised when the mendicant burst into tears. Samudra said, "Kind sir, I grieve not for the destruction of this body, but for losing this hard-to-attain existence, in which I have been instructed by the lion of the Shaakyas and was hoping to achieve liberation." Samudra, begging for compassion, sought a month's delay of the execution. Chandagirikaa granted him a seven-day reprieve. Samudra waited, wrestling with the fear of death.

It so happened that early on the seventh morning, Chandagirikaa met Samudra and said, "Monk, the night is gone, the sun has risen, the time of your torture has come." Calmly, Samudra replied, "True, my night of ignorance has cleared and the sun of my good fortune is at its height. You may do as you wish, my friend." Unmoved, the executioner threw Samudra into a cauldron full of water and blood and tried to light a fire underneath. Try as he might, the fire would not blaze. Puzzled, he looked into the vessel and was amazed to see the monk sitting calmly on a lotus within it. He rushed to Ashoka, who came to witness the miracle along with hundreds of people. Seeing the King, Samudra divined that the time had come for Ashoka's conversion.

Miraculously, Samudra floated up in the air and stunned the monarch.

For from half his body water poured down, from the other half, fire blazed forth, raining and flaming, he was shining in the sky. Seeing the miracle, Ashoka begged enlightenment and initiation into the mysteries of the Dharma of Samudra. Samudra then told Ashoka how the Buddha had predicted that a hundred years after his demise there would be in Pataliputra a king who would distribute his bodily relics in eighty four thousand stupas. "Instead, your majesty, you have built this palace which is hell and where thousands are tortured to death" said Samudra, 'O king, grant security to all beings, for compassion is the highest virtue. Fulfill the lord's prediction." Begging forgiveness, Ashoka proclaimed his faith in the Buddha, in the congregation of believers (*Sangha*) and in his teachings (*Dharma*). He also promised to adorn the earth with chaityas housing the Blessed One's relics. And that is how Ashoka came into the folds of Buddhism.

Another story goes as follows:

This was the time when Ashoka had not yet become a staunch follower of Buddhism. One day, looking out of the window, he saw a Buddhist monk named Nigrodha walking along. His face was serene. From the days of Ashoka's father, it was a tradition for the king to distribute food to hundreds of Brahmins. Ashoka decided to serve food to the Buddhist monk that day and sent for him. Nigrodha entered the palace. Nigrodha told him, he is a Buddhist monk and son of Sushima. Ashoka was shocked, because Sushima was his elder brother whom he had killed to become an emperor of Maurya dynasty. But Nigrodha showed neither anger nor hatred towards Ashoka and his face was calm and composed. He asked the monk to be seated in the court. Nigrodha looked around and did not find any seat empty except that of Emperor Ashoka. Nigrodha walked up to the throne and sat on it and Ashoka followed him back to his throne. There was no one there superior to the monk in status. He felt happy that Nigrodha had been accorded a seat befitting his worth. According to Buddhist principles, any member of the Buddha Sangha is accorded greater honour than the king. In this respect, the king has the second place.

Ashoka honoured Nigrodha by serving food and drinks. In return, Nigrodha delivered a discourse on Buddhism. The next day also Nigrodha, along with his disciples, received food from Ashoka. Again, Nigrodha gave a discourse on Buddhism. This went on for some time and Ashoka developed leanings towards Buddhism.

CHAPTER 12
The Basics of Buddhism

Buddhism is the religion, which brought about a incredible change in Ashoka. So the reader might be interested to know about the basics of the religion.

The following are the basics of the Buddhism in brief for the benefit of the reader.

The Four Noble Truths of Buddhism

- *All existence is dukkha* - Life is suffering. The Buddha's insight was that our lives are a struggle.
- *The cause of dukkha is craving* - Suffering is due to attachment. Buddha says that man's sufferings actual root is to be found in his own mind.
- *The cessation of dukkha comes with the cessation of craving* - Attachment can be overcome. As we are the ultimate cause of our difficulties, we are also the solution. We cannot change the things that happen to us, but we can change our responses.
- *There is a path that leads from dukkha* - There is a path for accomplishing this. Buddha taught methods

through which we can change ourselves, for example the Noble Eightfold Path.

The Eightfold Path

- *Right Understanding* : This is a significant step on the path as it relates to seeing the world and everything in it as it really is, not as we believe it to be or want it to be. Right view is the true understanding of the four noble truths.

- *Right Intent* : Right aspiration is the true desire to free oneself from attachment, ignorance and hatefulness. Right Understanding shows us what life really is and what life's problems are composed of, Right Intent urges us to decide what our heart wants. These two are referred to as prajna or wisdom.

- *Right Speech* : Right speech involves recognition of the truth, and also an awareness of the impact of idle gossip. Communicating thoughtfully helps to unite others, and can heal dissention.

- *Right Action* : Right Action recognises the need to take the ethical approach in life. This includes not taking what is not given to us, and having respect for the agreements we make both in our private and business lives. Right Action encompasses the five precepts which were given by the Buddha, not to kill, steal, lie, to avoid sexual misconduct, and not to take drugs or other intoxicants.

- *Right Livelihood* : Right livelihood means making your living in such a way as to avoid dishonesty and avoid dealing in such business which are harmful to both human and animal lives Buddhism promotes the principle of equality of all living beings and respect for all life.

These three are referred to as shila, or morality.

- *Right Effort* : Right Effort means cultivating an enthusiasm, a positive attitude in a balanced way. In order to produce Right Effort, clear and honest thoughts should be welcomed, and feelings of jealousy and anger left behind. Right Effort equates to positive thinking, followed by focused action.
- *Right Mindfulness* : Right Mindfulness means being aware of the moment, and being focused in that moment. By being aware, we are able to see how old patterns and habits control us. In this awareness, we may see how fears of possible futures limit our present actions.
- *Right Concentration* : Right concentration implies that we select worthy directions for the concentration of the mind. Right concentration is meditating in such a way as to progressively realise a true understanding of imperfection, impermanence, and non-separateness.

The last three are known as samadhi, or meditation.

The Four Exalted Dwellings or Brahma Vihara in Buddhism

- The disciple of the Noble Ones, Kalamas, who, *in this way, is devoid of coveting, devoid of ill will, undeluded, clearly comprehending and mindful,* dwells, having pervaded with the thought of amity, all corners of the universe; he dwells, having pervaded because of the existence in it of all living beings, everywhere, the entire world, with the great, exalted, boundless thought of amity that is free of hate or malice.

- He lives, having pervaded, *with the thought of compassion*, all corners of the universe; he dwells, having pervaded because of the existence in it of the living beings, everywhere, the entire world, with the great, exalted, boundless thought of compassion that is free of hate or malice.

- He lives, having pervaded, *with the thought of gladness*, all corners of the universe; he dwells, having pervaded because of the existence in it of all living beings, everywhere, the entire world, with the great, exalted, boundless thought of gladness that is free of hate or malice.

- He lives, having pervaded, with the thought of equanimity, all corners of the universe; he dwells, having pervaded because of the existence in it of all living beings, everywhere, the entire world, with the great, exalted, boundless thought of equanimity that is free of hate or malice.

The Four Solaces in Buddhism

The disciple of the Noble Ones, Kalamas, who has such a hate-free mind, such a malice-free mind, such an undefiled mind, and such a purified mind, is one by whom four solaces are found here and now.

- Suppose there is a hereafter and there is a fruit, result of deeds done well or ill. Then, it is possible that at the dissolution of the body after death, I shall arise in the heavenly world, which is possessed of the state of bliss.
- Suppose there is no hereafter and there is no fruit, no result, of deeds done well or ill. Yet in this world, here and now, free from hatred, free from malice, safe and sound, and happy, I keep myself.
- Suppose evil (results) befall an evildoer. I, however, think of doing evil to no one. Then, how can ill (results) affect me who do no evil deed?
- Suppose evil (results) do not befall an evildoer. Then I see myself purified in any case.

Ashoka worked hard to spread the message of Buddhism not only in India but in the other countries as well. Ashoka was in fact one of the greatest preacher of Buddhism in ancient India.

CHAPTER 13
Spreading the Message of Dharma

Ashoka did not think of the good of only his subjects, he thought of the good of all mankind. He wished to win the hearts of people and to serve the world through religion and through good will and good action. He decided to dedicate his energy and all his powers and wealth to this goal.

The first thing that Ashoka did to spread righteousness among his people was to undertake a pilgrimage. It took place two years after the Kalinga war. His pilgrimage started with his visit to Sambodhi, the holy place where Gautama, the Buddha breathed his last. He visited other holy places during the pilgrimage Ashoka has explained in his own words the purpose of his pilgrimage,

"To meet Brahmins and Shramanas and to give gifts to them. To meet the elders and to honour them with gifts of gold. To meet people and to preach the law of Dharma and to discuss Dharma." These were the important objects.

Ashoka was not content with visiting holy places. He believed that the message of Dharma should not become stagnant like standing water. He wanted it to spread within India and outside India, too. He wanted the people of the world to bathe in its pure steam and purify themselves. Therefore, he undertook a great task, which would be enduring. He got the laws of Dharma engraved on rocks and stone pillars, both inside and outside the country.

These inscriptions were related to Dharma, social ethics and moral living. Ashoka himself has proclaimed that his desire was that his message should reach the people of all lands and enable them to follow and propagate the Dharma for the welfare of the world. Such inscriptions can be seen even today, both in India and outside countries. In India, they have been discovered in Madhya Pradesh, Gujarat, Uttar Pradesh, Maharashtra, Orissa, Andhra Pradesh and at Siddapura of Chitradurga District, Koppala and Maski in Raichur District of Karnataka. Outside India, they have been found in Peshawar District in Pakistan as well as near Khandahar in Afghanistan and on the borders of Nepal.

CHAPTER 14
The Able Ruler

Apart from spreading the message of Dharma, Ashoka also proved to be an able administrator.

For the purpose of administering the kingdom well, he divided the empire into four provinces each under a prince or member of the royal family whose official status was that of a viceroy. Governors administering smaller units were selected from amongst the local people. The provincial ministers were powerful and could act as a check on the viceroy, and on various occasions, proved to be effective rulers. Ashoka sent inspectors on tour every five years, for an additional audit and check on provincial administration. There were specially appointed judicial officers both in the cities and in the rural areas. Fines served as punishments in most cases. But certain crimes were considered too serious to be punished by fines alone and capital punishments were delivered.

Each province was sub-divided into districts, each of these into groups of villages, and the final unit of administration was the village. The group of villages was staffed with an accountant, who maintained boundaries, registered land and deeds, kept a census of the population and a record of the livestock; and a tax collector, who was concerned with the various types of revenue. Each village had its own officials, such as the headman, who was responsible to the accountant and the tax collector. Officers at this level in rural administration were paid either by a remission of tax or by land grants.

Urban administration had its own hierarchy of officers. The city superintendent maintained law and order and the general cleanliness of the city. Cities were generally built of wood, necessitating the maintaining of fire precautions. The city superintendent was assisted by an accountant and a tax collector. Megasthenes has described the administration of Pataliputra in detail. The city was administered by thirty officials, divided into six committees of five. Each committee supervised one of the following functions, namely questions relating to industrial arts, the welfare of foreigners, the registering of births and deaths, matters relating to trade and commerce, supervision of the public sale of manufactured goods and, finally, collection of the tax on articles sold.

Two of the key offices controlled by the central administration were those of the Treasurer and the chief collector. The Treasurer was responsible for keeping an account of the income in cash and for storing the income in kind. The Chief Collector, assisted by a body of clerks, kept records of the taxes, which came in from various parts of the empire. The accounts of every administrative department were properly kept and were presented jointly by all the ministers to the king, perhaps to avoid fraud and embezzlement. Each department had a large staff of superintendents and subordinate officers. The superintendents worked at local centre and were a link between local administration and the central government. Those specifically listed in the Arthashastra are the superintendents of gold and goldsmiths, and of the storehouse, commerce, forest produce, the armoury, weights and measures, tools, weaving, agriculture, liquor, slaughter houses, prostitutes, ships, cows, horses, elephants, chariots, infantry, passports and the city.

Salaries of officials and expenditure on public works constituted a sizeable portion of the national expenses, one quarter of the total revenue being reserved for these. The higher officials were extremely well paid and this must have been a drain on the treasury. The chief minister, the purohita and the army commander received 48,000 panas, the treasurer and the chief collector 24,000 panas; the accountants and clerks received 500 panas, whereas the ministers were paid 12,000 panas; and artisans received 120 panas. The value of the pana is not indicated, nor the intervals at which the salaries were paid.

CHAPTER 15
The Seeds of Dharma

We read in history about many kings who put up inscriptions about their invasions, charities, donations and the extension of their territories. But, it is only Ashoka who got inscriptions carved on rocks and pillars, which lead people from untruth to truth, from death to immortality and from darkness to light. To this day, they are like lights of wisdom. The laws of Dharma are like the seeds of virtue sown in the hearts of the people. They are steps leading to salvation.

Ashoka had engraved his Dharma, i.e., the 'Law of Piety' on the rocks and pillars in order to spread Buddhism. It contained the fundamental principles of mastery of the sense, purity of thought, gratitude, steadfastness of devotion, kindness, charity, purity, truthfulness, service, support and reverence.

In order to foster greater understanding regarding Dharma, Ashoka took a bold and firm step. He wished to show that all religions teach the same path of virtue. In one of his inscriptions, Ashoka says, "We must respect the followers of other religions in every way. By doing so, we can help the growth of our religion and we can help other religions also. If we act in a different way, it will harm our religion as well as the other religions. The man who wants his religion to spread rapidly and honours only his religion and speaks ill of other religions, will harm the interests of his own religion. The power of all religions should grow. Devanampriya does not consider charity and worship more important than this."

He appointed officers, called 'Dharma Mahamatras', in order to spread these ideas among the people. These officers met people of different religions and lived among them.

They helped to remove the mistaken ideas they had about other religions and to know what was good in them. Often, the money set apart for religious purposes was spent otherwise. Sometimes though, it seems to have been spent for religious purpose, but selfish people pocketed it. It was the duty of the Dharma Mahamatras to see that the money meant for religious purposes was spent properly. They toured the empire and visited the courts of justice also. They set right the errors in the conduct of affairs and in the awards of punishments. Such officers do not seem to have been appointed anywhere else in the history of the world. Besides these, other officers also toured the empire once in five years, according to the orders of the emperor, and spread the Dharma among the people.

CHAPTER 16
The Buddhist Council

After seventeen years of Ashoka's rule, unfortunately, a difference of opinion arose among the Buddhist monks and there was a split. The conversion of Emperor Ashoka to Buddhism in the expansion of his kingdom led to the patronisation of Buddhist activities. As a result of the encouragement, a lot of non-Buddhists joined the order not because of their interest but for royal patronage. There were many lazy and bad monks given to evil ways. These willful sanyasis were a curse to Buddhism. Buddhism was, therefore, losing its power. Ashoka felt unhappy over this. In order to save Buddhism from total eclipse and to increase its influence, Ashoka threw out many lazy monks from the Buddhist fold. He invited the worthy and the serious - minded monks to Ashokarama in Pataliputra for a conference, which is known as the third Buddhist Council.

It has to be mentioned here that prior to Ashoka, two Buddhist Councils were held in India. The early Buddhist councils were mainly concerned with the purity of the

faith and practice of the monastic community. For five hundred years after the Buddha's Nirvana, his teaching and discipline were retained in the memories of monks who periodically assembled to recite and review them.

It was not until the fourth council that the valuable knowledge had finally been preserved with written format.

The third council called by Ashoka was presided over by Moggaliputra Tishya and attended by the Buddhist monks from the Four Corners of the country. Ashoka sat with the great teaches and sent for each Bhikshu and asked him, "What did Lord Buddha teach?" He discussed many things with them. After long discussions, what Lord Buddha had taught came out clearly and unambiguously. The council also compiled the Buddhist teachings, for the first time, in three Buddhist canons (Tripitaka) and missionaries were sent out to various countries. The Tripitaka included Vinaya, Dharma and Abhidharma. The new canon, Abhidharma, covering Buddhist Philosophy and Psychology, was essentially compiled to clarify some differences found in Vinaya and Dharma.

Buddhism gained a new strength from this conference. Ashoka did not, like other kings, send his armies to foreign lands to conquer them. He who declared that the victory of Dharma was the real victory, sent Buddhist monks to other lands, the light he had received from Buddhism. He sent Buddhist preachers to Syria, Egypt, Macedonia, Burma and Kashmir. To Ceylon (Srilanka), he sent his own children Mahendra and Sanghamitra. As a result of this, Buddhism spread to all countries in East Asia.

CHAPTER 17
The Second Pilgrimage

In the twentieth year of his reign, Ashoka undertook his second pilgrimage with his daughter and Upagupta. This, we learn from his inscriptions. During this pilgrimage, he visited the ruins of Vaishali, and the places where Buddha used to rest. From Vaishali, Ashoka travelled east and came to Ramagrama. He visited the Stupa (A stupa is a sacred place where the mortal remains of Buddha are kept for worship) at Ramagrama, built by a king who had collected and preserved the sacred bones of Buddha after his death. Later he also visited Lumbini, Kapilavastu, Shravanti, Gaya and other holy places. Wherever he went, he caused pillars and stupas to be erected in memory of his visit. They remind us even today of the visit of Ashoka to those holy places.

There is one such memorial pillar at Sarnath. On the top of a stone pillar, about fifty feet high, there are beautifully carved figures of four standing lions. The figures of the lions are now to be seen in the official emblem of the government of free India, and the 24 spokes Ashoka

Chakra adorns the national flag of India. In this way, the government of India has paid a deserving tribute to the ideal king, Ashoka.

But, unfortunately, the pillar at Sarnath is broken and mutilated. So today, only fragments of the pillar are to be seen. Of the eighty-four thousand stupas built by Ashoka, the stupa at Sanchi is both famous and splendid.

To this day, this fifty-four feet stupa stands on a high pedestal and forms a semicircle. Besides these stupas and pillars, Ashoka built cave dwellings, rest houses and Buddha Viharas in large numbers. They not only proclaim Ashoka's teachings but also are examples of the splendid architecture of those days.

CHAPTER 18
The People's Friend

There have been many emperors in the history of India but few ruled over such a vast empire as Ashoka's. His empire extended over a large part of India, Afghanistan and Balochistan, beyond the Northwest province and Nepal in the North, as well as the Bengal, Bihar, Andhra Pradesh and a large part of Karnataka of today. The inscriptions discovered in these parts prove this.

But Ashoka was not vain; he ruled his kingdom very ably. In fact, he was called 'the People's friend'. Ashoka continued the ideal and the tradition of his grandfather Chandragupta and practiced, in letter and spirit, the routine set down by Kautilya. Kautilya, the Chief Minister of Chandragupta Maurya, has described the daily life of the kings of that age.

According to Kautaliya's Arthashastra, a King had very exhausting schedule where they slept only for four and a half hours. So, a Mauryan King divided his 24 hours into 16 periods of one and a half hours each, and would perform his duties as mentioned in the Time Table below:

A mauryan king would get up at 1.30 am

Life of the Mauryan King was not as easy as other kings, perhaps that is why they could rule the Kingdom so well. A Mauryan king would get up at 1.30 am in the morning, and meditate for around one and a half hours with respect to the day's work.

From 3 am to 4.30 am, the king would strategize political matters

The Mauryan King examines various political matters, discuss the daily important matters with his councilors, and would then send his spies to various corners of his empire.

4.30 am to 6.00 am was dedicated to meetings

The next one and a half hour was strictly dedicated to meeting. The King made sure he carried out his duties including household, religious and personal duties effectively. During this period, he met advisors, teachers and priests to discuss matters on rituals. He also met his personal doctor, the royal astrologer along with the royal cook.

6.00 am to 7.30 am is spent in the court hall

During this hour after sunrise is quite vital as during this period the King receives all the reports regarding revenue, and expenditure of the previous day.

7.30 am to 9.00 am is hearing time

During time the king hears the petition of his people who come from his own town as well as other cities in his kingdom. He hears their petition and addresses the public grievances.

9.00 to 10.30 am is king's personal time

During this period, Mauryan King would take bath, pray and then have breakfast. This hour is purely his time where nobody disturbs him.

From 10.30 am to noon is the time of allotment

During this time the Kings would appoint the officials, ministers and even allot different types of task to them.

From 12.00 pm to 1.30 pm is the time of council of ministers

This is conference time with the King and his Council of Ministers regarding introducing new policies or amending the existing policies.

1.30 pm to 3 pm is king's recreation time!

3 pm to 4.30 pm is defense time

During this time, the Mauryan Kings would inspect the forces, talk to the Senapati, the Chief of the Defense and review everything related to the matters of Defense.

Later, during the time of sunset, the Mauryan King would spend his time in Prayers. From 6.00 pm to 7.30 pm he would meet his spies, who would come from various parts of the kingdom. From 7.30 pm to 9.00 pm he would spend time in having bath, eating dinner and studying. At 9.00 pm he would retire for the night and would get up at 1.30 am to meditate.

Besides, Ashoka believed that the prosperity of his subjects was his prosperity, so he had appointed officers to

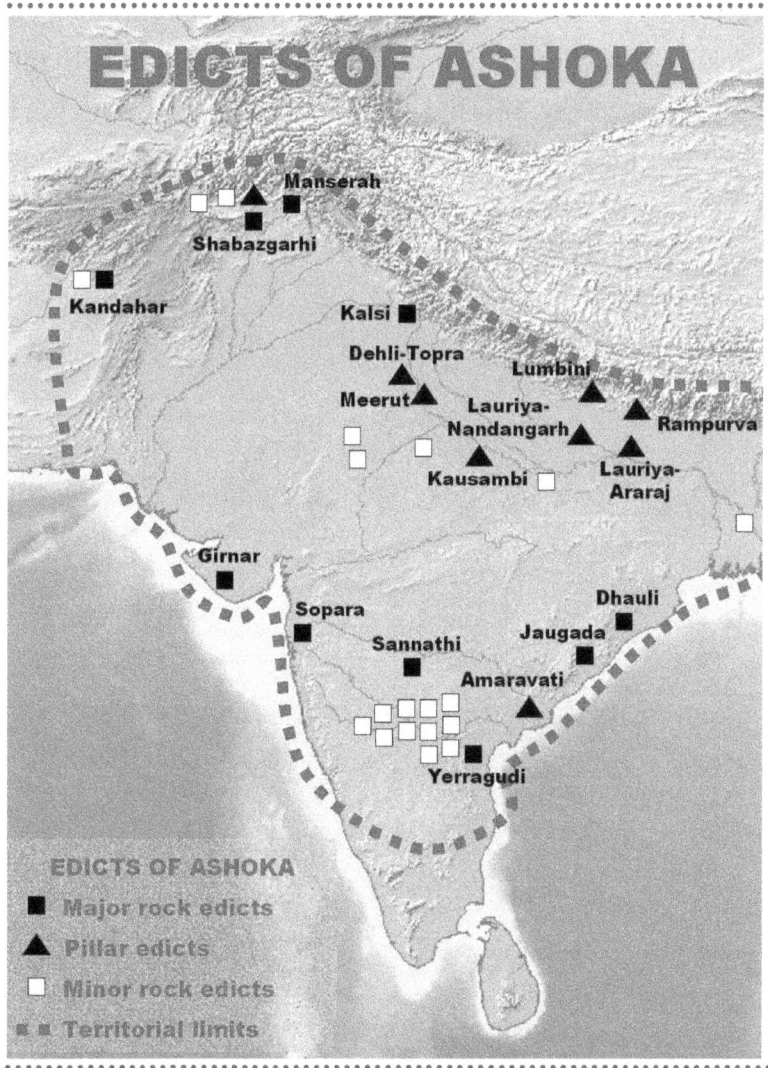

report to him on the welfare and sufferings of the people. They were to report to him no matter what the hour was. His own order best shows his concern for the people, "Whether 1 am dining or in my private apartments, asleep or engaged in some work, setting out on a journey or resting; wherever I may be and whatever the time of the day or night, the officers must come and report to me about the people and their affairs. Wherever I may be, I shall think about the welfare of the people and work for them." These words are enough to show Ashoka's devotion towards the welfare of his people.

CHAPTER 19
The Proficient Ruler

Ashoka was a very proficient ruler who devoted his lifetime as a king for the all round development of his kingdom and his subjects. Ashoka worked hard, especially for the spread of education in his land. Malinda is famous in history, it, was the centre of education and the University of Magadha. It is said to have founded by Ashoka. Students of this university were very much respected. During his time, trading with foreign countries was carried on by sea routes.

He encouraged agriculture, trade and industries. There were canals to help irrigation. All the money paid into the government treasury was spent for the welfare of the people.

Ashoka had big roads laid to help the growth of business and industries. For the benefit of travelers, he had trees planted on both sides of the roads. Wells were dug and guest houses and rest houses were put up. There was free medical aid, both for men and for animals. Ashoka was among the first in the world to build hospitals for the treatment of animals. He got medicinal plants and a variety of fruit-bearing trees from several places and planted them where they were not found. In one inscription, he has expressed the wish that even the forest dwellers in his empire should live happily.

Sandalwood wears itself out to give a cool and fragrant paste to men. Sugarcane gives up its sweet juice to men and reduces itself to mere skin in the process. The candle burns itself out that others may have light. All his life, Ashoka lived like the sandal wood, the sugarcane and like the candle.

He worked hard without rest and taught the people to live a life of truthfulness, Dharma, Justice and morality. There was happiness and peace. There were social gatherings at which people of all castes and creeds gathered and enjoyed themselves, without any feeling of high and low.

CHAPTER 20
The Last Days

Ashoka, who was the embodiment of pity, kindness and love, unfortunately had to suffer much in his old age. The reason for this was - his sons, Mahendra, Kunala and Tivala were engaged in spreading Buddhism and so, his grandsons Dasharatha and Samprati started quarrelling over the right of succession to the throne. Even the queens quarreled over the issue. There was one among them, Tishyarakshite, who was a wicked woman. Ashoka was a monk among kings and had given up all pomp and pleasures and lived a very simple life. This did not please Tishyarakshite who loved the life of ease and comfort.

Moreover, the young Tishyaraksha hated the old king and had an eye for his young son, Prince Kunala. The Prince was, on the other hand, very pained with her conduct and left for Taxila with his wife, never to return or claim the throne. All this made Ashoka very sad and condemned Tishyaraksha to death, restoring Kunala to the court. By this time, he had grown old. Not much is known about the last ten years of his life and about his death. Some say that the emperor got disgusted in life and therefore, he went on a pilgrimage as a Buddhist monk with his teacher, for the peace of his mind. At last, he reached Taxila and stayed there. Ashoka, the beloved of Gods and men, left the earth at the age of seventy-two. However, it is clear that Ashoka was unhappy in his old age.

CHAPTER 21
The Generous King

Ashoka was a generous king and apart from giving donations to his subjects, he also donated large sums of money and goods to the Buddhist Sangha.

During his old age, Ashoka was keen to be the greatest of all donors to the Faith of the Buddha. He enquired of the monks who had been, so far, the greatest donor. They informed him that it was the householder Anaathapindada who had gifted the Sangha one hundred crore gold pieces. Ashoka wished to do likewise. He had, until then, gifted ninety-six crore by building the stupas and chaityas, holding the five year festival, etc.

But when Ashoka's health began to fail, he became sad, fearing that he would be unable to fulfill his resolve. He therefore began sending gold coins regularly to the monastery at Kukkutaraama.

By that time, Kunala's son Sampadin had become the crown prince. His advisors told him that the king was draining the state treasury and ought to be controlled.

Sampadin, there upon ordered the treasurer not to give out state funds.

When Ashoka heard about this, he began to send the golden plates on which his food was brought, to the monastery, as offerings. Sampadin extended the ban to this too. Ashoka began to be served on silver dishes. He sent these as well to the Sangha. When copper replaced silver and then by clay plates, the king persisted in dispatching those to Kukkutaraama.

Finally, a day came when all that Ashoka had left was half of an 'amlaka' fruit. Taking it in his hand, Ashoka then called a passer-bye and said, "My friend, though I have fallen from power, do this last task for me, out of regard for my past virtues. Take this, my half-'amlaka', and offer it to the monastery on my behalf, saying, 'I offer you the present greatness of the king who ruled all of Jambudveepa' and request to have it so distributed that it is enjoyed by the whole community of monks."

The citizen faithfully performed his duty and offered the half of the fruit to the monastery saying, "He who previously ruled the earth, warming it like the sun at noon, today he is deceived by his karmic acts and finds his glory gone like the setting sun at dusk."

The head of the monastery then had the half 'amlaka' mashed, put in a soup and distributed to the entire Sangha of monks.

Emperor Ashoka then struggled to his feet, gazed in the four directions and announced, "Except for the state treasury, I give to the Sangha this earth, with its Mandara mountain and its dark blue garment, the ocean, and its face adorned with many jewels. With this gift, I do not seek any rebirth in heaven or even less on earth as a king. Because I give it with faith, I would obtain as its fruit, something that cannot be stolen, that which is honoured by the Aryas and safe from all flux, sovereignty over the mind."

Ashoka inscribed this and sealed it with his teeth and then passed away. When the ministers prepared to install Sampadin as king, Radhagupta reminded them that Ashoka had gifted the whole kingdom away. When

the ministers were at a loss, Radhagupta told them that it had been Ashoka's desire to donate one hundred crore gold coins to the Sangha and that when he died ninety-six crore had been gifted. It was to complete his intention that he had gifted the kingdom. Thereupon the ministers gave four crore gold coins to the Sangha and redeemed the kingdom to bless Sampadin as the new king.

CHAPTER 22
The Decline of Mauryan Empire

Ashoka ruled for 37 years and died in 232 B.C. With his death, political decline set in and soon after, the empire broke up. The Ganges valley remained under the Mauryas for another fifty years. The north-western areas were lost to the Bactrian Greeks by about 180 B.C.

The reasons for this political decline are, up to a point, similar in the disintegration of most empires on the Indian sub-continent. The political and administrative causes are that Ashoka was succeeded by weak rulers. This encouraged the provinces to proclaim their independence. The weak rulers could not execute the arduous task of administering such a vast empire. The mutual quarrel among the successors also contributed to the decline of the Mauryan Empire.

Among the religious causes, historians say that Ashoka had invoked a strong religious doctrine based on the law of piety. The policy of peace during the rule of Ashoka was mainly due to his influence over the vast empire.

The Brahmanas who, before the Mauryas, had contributed to the establishment of the Mauryan rule, now organised to the establishment of the old order. This quelled the impact of the Buddhist doctrine, which was made a political, economic and social policy, besides influencing the cultural sphere of the life during the Ashokan period. Some people carried on false propaganda that Ashoka was partial to Buddhism and was contemptuous towards other religions. So, some sections of the people turned against the emperor.

The inactive army, whose officers were made Dharma Mahamantras for propagating the law of piety, lost their skill to defend themselves.

But making these factors, singly responsible for the decline of the Mauryan Empire, would be an exaggeration

of facts. Mauryan economy was under considerable pressure. The need for vast revenues to maintain the army and to finance the salaries of officials and settlements on newly cleared land must have strained the treasury.

Hence Vastness of the Empire, Weak Successors of Ashoka, Independence of the Provinces, Internal Revolt and various religious causes were the major reason for the downfall of Mauryan dynasty.

By 180 B.C., the first experiment in imperial government in India had ended. Other experiments were to be made in later centuries, but the conditions were never quite the same.

CHAPTER 23
Ashoka the Shining Star

Ashoka has been called as 'Devanampriya' and Priyadarshi' in his inscriptions. 'Devanampriya' means the beloved of the Gods and Priyadarshi means one whose appearance brings joy. These names are appropriate to Ashoka's nature. The Gods without doubt love a man of such virtues. There was no one to check him, no one to punish him if he did wrong. But, he became, his own teacher and checked his desires. He dedicated his life to the happiness and welfare of his people. It is no wonder that he was loved so much by his subjects.

Some historians say that Ashoka followed the teachings of Buddhism so devotedly that he himself became a Buddhist monk. Though he was the emperor, he probably often stayed in the Viharas. When he stayed in Viharas, he used to observe fast like the monk, very strictly, and also followed the religious practices. During his stay there, he learnt the teachings of Buddha in great detail.

Ashoka passed away from this world two thousand years ago, but his empire of truthfulness, Dharma, non-violence, compassion and love of subjects has remained as shining ideals for the world to this day. His Empire of love is immortal. Therefore, an English historian, has said, "In the history of the world, there have been thousands of kings and emperors who called themselves 'Their Highnesses', 'Their Majesties' and 'Their Exalted Majesties' and so on. They shone for a brief movement and disappeared. But, Ashoka shines and shines brightly like a bright star even today." This praise is fully merited.

In the long history of mankind, there is not another name equal to that of Ashoka. The great historian and authoritarian on Indian History and Law, Dr. Radhakumuda Mukherjee said, "In the history of royal families, there is none to equal the record of Ashoka, both as a person and as a king."

The rule of Ashoka establishes itself as the most attractive chapter in the history of India. Ashoka was the only emperor to follow a path of peace and Dharma after a great military victory. As a teacher of religious tolerance and universal fraternity, he stands alone. Ashoka was perhaps the 'primary internationalist' of the world.

CHAPTER 24
Edicts of Ashok

Ashoka (304-232 B.C.) was third king of the Mauryan dynasty and is regarded by many as the most exemplary ruler of the ancient world. He left his preachings for posterity in the edicts, in the beautiful carvings of pillars and rocks that he built throughout his empire. The texts, which follow, are excerpts from his 'Rock Edicts' and 'Pillar Edicts', so-called because they were inscribed on rocks and stone pillars to make them public.

- Here (In my domain), no living beings are to be slaughtered or offered in sacrifice. Nor should festivals be held, for Beloved-of-the-Gods, King Priyadarshi, sees much to object to in such festivals, although there are some festivals that Beloved-of-the-Gods, King Priyadarshi, does approve of.
- Everywhere within Beloved-of-the-Gods, King Priyadarshi's domain, and among the people beyond the borders, the Cholas, the Pandyas, the Satiyaputras, the Keralaputras, as far as Tamraparni and where the

Greek king Antiochos rules, and among the kings who are neighbours of Antiochos, everywhere has Beloved-of-the-Gods, King Priyadarshi, made provision for two types of medical treatment: medical treatment for humans and medical treatment for animals. Wherever medical herbs suitable for humans or animals are not available, I have had them imported and grown. Along roads, I have had wells dug and trees planted for the benefit of humans and animals.

- Beloved-of-the-Gods, King Priyadarshi, desires that all religions should reside everywhere, for all of them desire self-control and purity of heart. But people have various desires and various passions, and they may practice all of what they should or only a part of it. But one who receives great gifts yet is lacking in self-control, purity of heart, gratitude and firm devotion, such a person is mean.

- Ten years after Beloved-of-the-Gods had been crowned, he went on a tour to Sambodhi and thus instituted Dhamma tours. During these tours, the following things took place: visits and gifts to Brahmans and ascetics, visits and gifts of gold to the aged, visits to people in the countryside, instructing them in Dhamma, and discussing Dhamma with them as is suitable. It is this that delights Beloved-of-the-Gods, King Priyadarshi, and is, as it were, another type of revenue.

- Beloved-of-the-Gods, King Priyadarshi, conquered the Kalingas eight years after his coronation. One hundred and fifty thousand were deported, one hundred thousand were killed and many more died (from other causes). After the Kalingas had been conquered, Beloved-of-the-Gods came to feel a strong inclination towards the Dhamma, a love for the Dhamma and for instruction in Dhamma. Now, Beloved-of-the-Gods feels deep remorse for having conquered the Kalingas.
- Indeed, Beloved-of-the-Gods is deeply pained by the killing, dying and deportation that take place when an unconquered country is conquered. But Beloved-of-the-Gods is pained even more by this - that Brahmans, ascetics, and householders of different religions who live in those countries, and who are respectful to superiors, to mother and father, to elders, and who behave properly and have strong loyalty towards friends, acquaintances, companions, relatives, servants and employees

- that they are injured, killed or separated from their loved ones.
- There is no country, except among the Greeks, where these two groups, Brahmans and ascetics, are not found, and there is no country where people are not devoted to one or another religion. Therefore, the killing, death or deportation of a hundredth, or even a thousandth part of those who died during the conquest of Kalinga now pains Beloved-of-the-Gods. Now, Beloved-of-the-Gods thinks that even those who do wrong, should be forgiven where forgiveness is possible.
- I have had this Dhamma edict written so that my sons and great-grandsons may not consider making new conquests or that if military conquests are made,  that they be done with forbearance and light punishment, or better still, that they consider making conquest by Dhamma only, for that bears fruit in this world and the next. May all their intense devotion be given to this, which has a result in this world and into the next.

www.ingramcontent.com/pod-product-compliance
Lightning Source LLC
LaVergne TN
LVHW091317080426
835510LV00007B/523